Why You Should Become A Professional Coach

Professional Coaching has been a real growth profession since the 1990s.

In this book you will learn what Professional Coaching is all about and how to make a decision if it is for you.

We will answer questions you might have like:

- Is Coaching a real profession?
- What types of Coaches are there?
- Can I make a good living at Coaching?
- What do I need to do to succeed?
- What issues should I be careful about?
- What is Virtual Coaching?
- How is Coaching Age Dependent?

I hope you enjoy the book and it helps you make decisions about your career.

Why You Should Become A Professional Coach

Why You Should Become A Professional Coach

Copyright Page

Why You Should Become a Professional Coach

By Martin K. Ettington

The Professional Coaching Series Book 1

Why You Should Become A
Professional Coach

Why You Should Become A Professional Coach

Other books by Martin K. Ettington

Why You Should Become A
Professional Coach

Real Time Travel Stories From a Psychic Engineer

Removing Limits On Our Consciousness-And Thinking Outside the Box

33 Incredible True Survival Stories

How to Survive Anything: From the Wilderness to Man Made Disasters

Building and Stocking a Nuclear Shelter for less than $10,000

All About Mars Journeys and Settlement

Mining the Asteroid Belt

Ancient History

The Real Atlantis-In the Eye of the Sahara

Ancient & Prehistoric Civilizations

Ancient & Prehistoric Civilizations-Book Two

The History of Antediluvian Giants

The Antediluvian History of Earth

Ancient Underground Cities and Tunnels

Strange Objects Which Should Not Exist

Strange and Ancient Places in the USA

A Theory of Ancient Prehistory And Giant Aliens

Aliens and Space

Aliens and Secret Technology

Aliens Are Already Among Us

Designing and Building Space Colonies

Humanity and the Universe

All About Moon Bases

All About Mars Journeys and Settlement

The Space and Aliens Six Books Bundle

A Theory of Ancient Prehistory and Giant Aliens

The Space Colonies and Space Structures Coloring Book

All About Asteroids

Spaceships, Past, Present, and Future

The Longevity Training Series

(A transcription of the online Multimedia Longevity Coaching Training Program)

The Personal Longevity Training Series-Book1-Long Lived Persons
The Personal Longevity Training Series-Book2-Your Soul's Purpose
The Personal Longevity Training Series-Book3-Enable Your Life Urge
The Personal Longevity Training Series-Book4-Your Spiritual Connection
The Personal Longevity Training Series-Book5-Having Love in Your Heart
The Personal Longevity Training Series-Book6-Energy Body Health
The Personal Longevity Training Series-Book7-The Science of Longevity
The Personal Longevity Training Series-Book8-Physical Body Health
The Personal Longevity Training Series-Book9-Avoiding Accidents
The Personal Longevity Training Series-Book10-Implementing These Principles

The Personal Longevity Training Series-Books One Thru Ten

These books are all available in digital and printed formats from my website and on Amazon, Barnes & Noble, Apple ITunes, and many other sites

My Books Website is: http://mkettingtonbooks.com

Why You Should Become A Professional Coach

Signup for our Mailing List to get the following:

1) A discount coupon for 25% discount on all books on our site

2) Occasional Notices of new books available

3) Occasional Email on other offerings of ours (Monthly)

Go to this link to sign-up:

http://personal-longevity.com/mkebooks/emailsignup/

And click this link to get the FREE 102 page Ebook titled "Secrets of Many Things"

If you have any questions about this book or other subjects please contact the Author at:

mke@mkettingtonbooks.com

Why You Should Become A Professional Coach

Why You Should Become A Professional Coach

Table of Contents

Why You Should Become A Professional Coach

Why You Should Become A Professional Coach

Chapter 1: Introduction

Hello and welcome to this book on Professional Coaching.

My name is Marty Ettington and I developed Longevity Coaching as a type of professional coaching back in 2013.

I now sell it in North America and Internationally—and am gaining a big following.

People often ask me these questions:

- Is Coaching a real profession?
- Is your Coaching program certified?
- Can I really make money as a Professional Coach?

Having researched the market extensively before I got into it, I have a lot of information about the professional coaching market.

After doing a search on Amazon.com recently I also realized there weren't any books addressing the "Whys" and history of professional coaching.

Everyone seems to assume we all know what professional coaching is all about.

I've met many coaches who make over half a million dollars a year. The sky seems to be the limit—if you know what you are doing.

And professional coaching is a fast growing profession.

So I'm going to share what I've learned about this fascinating market—and I'll "Blow my own horn" too. ☺

Why You Should Become A
Professional Coach

Why You Should Become A Professional Coach

A BRIEF HISTORY OF COACHING

Chapter 2: The History of and Types of Coaching:

If you really want to go back in time you can probably go all the way back to the nineteenth century. Here is a quote on the development of professional coaching:

> *The first use of the term "coach" in connection with an instructor or trainer arose around 1830 in Oxford University slang for a tutor who "carried" a student through an exam. The word "coaching" thus identified a process used to transport people from where they are to where they want to be. The first use of the term in relation to sports came in 1861. Historically the development of coaching has been influenced by many fields of activity, including adult education, the Human Potential Movement, large-group awareness training (LGAT) groups such as "est", leadership studies, personal development, and psychology.*

The 20th century saw a lot of professions develop which were at their most basic a type of coaching. These professions included:

- Psychologists
- Psychiatrists

- Personal Therapists
- Sports Coaching

Then in the 1990s, the types of professional coaches grew and fragmented as people identified more and more diverse needs. Here are some of the new major categories of professional coaching:

ADHD Coaching

The concept of ADHD coaching was first introduced in 1994 by psychiatrists Edward M. Hallowell and John J. Ratey in their book Driven to Distraction. ADHD coaching is a specialized type of life coaching that uses specific techniques designed to assist individuals with attention-deficit hyperactivity disorder. The goal of ADHD coaching is to mitigate the effects of executive function deficit, which is a typical impairment for people with ADHD

Business Coaching

Business coaching is a type of human resource development for business leaders. It provides positive support, feedback and advice on an individual or group basis to improve personal effectiveness in the business setting. Business coaching is also called executive coaching, corporate coaching or leadership coaching. Coaches help their clients advance towards specific professional goals. These include career transition, interpersonal and professional communication, performance management, organizational effectiveness, managing career and personal changes, developing executive presence, enhancing strategic thinking, dealing effectively with conflict, and building an effective team within an organization.

Why You Should Become A Professional Coach

Career Coaching

Career coaching focuses on work and career and is similar to career counseling. Career coaching is not to be confused with life coaching, which concentrates on personal development. Another common term for a career coach is career guide.

Christian Coaching

Christian coaching is common among religious organizations and churches. A Christian coach is not a pastor or counselor (although he may also be qualified in those disciplines), but rather someone who has been professionally trained to address specific coaching goals from a distinctively Christian or biblical perspective. Although various training courses exist, there is no single regulatory body for Christian coaching. Some of the Christian coaching programs are based on the works of Henry Cloud, John Townsend, and John C. Maxwell

Financial Coaching

Financial coaching is a relatively new form of coaching that focuses on helping clients overcome their struggle to attain specific financial goals and aspirations they have set for themselves. Financial coaching is a one-on-one relationship in which the coach works to provide encouragement and support aimed at facilitating attainment of the client's financial plans. A financial coach, also called money coach, typically focuses on helping clients to restructure and reduce debt, reduce spending, develop saving habits, and develop financial discipline. In contrast, the term financial adviser refers to a wider range of professionals who typically provide clients with financial products and services.

Why You Should Become A Professional Coach

Health & Wellness Coaching

My Longevity Coaching program is a type of Health Coaching.

Health coaching is becoming recognized as a new way to help individuals "manage" their illnesses and conditions, especially those of a chronic nature. The coach will use special techniques, personal experience, expertise and encouragement to assist the coaches in bringing his/her behavioral changes about, while aiming for lowered health risks and decreased healthcare costs.

The National Society of Health Coaches (NSHC) has differentiated the term health coach from wellness coach. According to the NSHC, health coaches are qualified "to guide those with acute or chronic conditions and/or moderate to high health risk", and wellness coaches provide guidance and inspiration "to otherwise 'healthy' individuals who desire to maintain or improve their overall general health status".

Since many wellness specialists also do coaching I would expand this focus to include:

- Massage Therapists
- Chiropractors
- Reiki Healers
- Yoga Meditation Instructors
- Diet Coaching
- Nutrition Coaching
- Exercise Coaching

Homework Coaching

Homework coaching focuses on equipping a student with the study skills required to succeed academically. This approach is different from regular tutoring which typically seeks to improve a student's performance in a specific subject.

Why You Should Become A Professional Coach

Homework coaching focuses on equipping a student with the study skills required to succeed academically. This approach is different from regular tutoring which typically seeks to improve a student's performance in a specific subject

Life Coaching

This type of Coaching is often about Life Purpose and Goals definition along with what motivates the client. It can also include coaching on the clients professional areas too.

Longevity Coaching can also fit in this niche.

Relationship Coaching

This is the process of counseling the parties of a human relationship in an effort to recognize, and to better manage or reconcile, troublesome differences and repeating patterns of stress upon the relationship. The relationship involved may be between members of a family, or a couple, employees or employers in a workplace, or between a professional and a client.

Sports Coaching

In **sports**, a coach is an individual that provides supervision and training to the sports team or individual players. Sports coaches are involved in administration, athletic training, competition coaching, and representation of the team and the players.

Team Facilitation

Coaching in its role as facilitator is particularly valuable during the budget and strategy planning season. And coaching a team before a presentation can dramatically improve performance – as well as self confidence

Work Shadowing

As well as being a means of identifying an individual's behavior and performance, work shadowing is an excellent method of getting immediate feedback on behavior, with a discussion of alternative ways of handling future such situations

There are other ways to define Coaching by whether it is individual or group coaching, and the type of group being coached.

Whew! That is a lot of choices for coaching

My own opinion is that professional coaches can be as diverse as there are personalities.

In fact the Coaches I've met who are most successful can't be put into one of the above categories.

What they do is so unique that it defies categorization. And these are the people who earn outrageous amounts of money—from satisfied clients.

I know one guy here in Los Angeles who earns over half a million a year working with clients individually and discussing what type of reality they live in. Of course I'm over simplifying, but what he does cannot be easily described.

Why You Should Become A Professional Coach

Chapter 3: Is Coaching a Real Profession?

People have asked me this question many times when discussing Longevity Coaching.

What is a real profession? To me it's one where you can earn a living.

Remember that the professions we recognize today were just off the cuff work in the past.

Health Coaching in general is a good example. I never heard of it before the year 2000. Now you can search job listings and find lots of them for "Health Coaches"

So if you feel confident in the skills you can offer clients, and that you can build a business out of offering those skills—that is all you really need.

Many people in today's world wide economy have a "Personal Brand" where they market themselves based on their individual skillsets.

"Personal Brand" is all about what are the unique skills you can offer your clients that distinguishes you from anyone else.

One gal I knew was a Photographer and Life Coach. Her brand was shooting before and after pictures of her clients to show how they had changed for the better as a result of her coaching practice.

You might call this "Coaching" or some type of "Consulting" but the basic rule is: Can you make a living doing this?

If you can—then it's a viable profession. If not—then you should find something else to do.

Chapter 4: How Much do Professional Coaches Earn?

I've met many professional coaches here in the Los Angeles area who regularly earn $500,000 to one million dollars per year.

Admittedly these people are at the tops of their professions.

In the year 2012 there were approximately 47,500 professional coaches at work that bring in a combined $2 billion in revenue. As an industry, Coaching is thriving.

What type of coaches are they? They are very diverse and hard to quantify but each person has a unique "Brand Identity" which gives them a high value to their clients.

Surveys by the National Academy of Coaching show that the average income for professional coaches is over $83,000 per year. (2012)

Recent findings in the 2011 Sherpa Study are that average annual incomes for coaches range from $55K to $116K

Coaches earn from $25 to $300 per hour. Average rates are $100 to $150 per hour. The more established coaches can charge up to $600 per hour.

Different types of Life Coaching and Corporate Coaching are the most lucrative. (I would call Longevity Coaching a type of Life Coaching)

Why You Should Become A Professional Coach

One Study says this about Coaching earnings:

The salary you make as a coach is determined by factors such as the type of coaching you do, your location and other factors such as how you position yourself against the competition. If you are like most people, you want to maximize your profit as a coach.

Chapter 5: What Standards & Risks Exist for Coaching?

Over time, different professions become established and have standards which are accepted by certification organizations—independent or governmental.

Engineering is a good example of when a focus of work became a profession. Engineering in some form has been practiced since Ancient times. However, professional certification for engineers didn't really exist until the 19th century. Electrical Engineering became a real profession in the late 1800s.

The status of most types of modern coaching is that these standards do not exist at the Federal or State level.

Here is what one source says about the standards for coaching:

> *While coaching has become a recognized intervention, sadly there are still no standards or licensing arrangements which are widely recognized. Professional bodies have continued to develop their own standards, but the lack of regulation means anyone can call themselves a coach. Whether coaching is a profession which requires regulation, or is professional and requires standards, remains a matter of debate.*

Although there are some professional organizations which offer "Coaching" certifications, after reading their websites I'm concerned about two things:

Why You Should Become A Professional Coach

1) Their certification program seems to be more of a continuous money making certification process—to generate a regular revenue stream for them from Coaching Providers

2) That some Coaching programs are "Out of the Box" like my Longevity Coaching program and they wouldn't have any way to decide if it was valid or not unless they took the Coaching program in question and were certified as a "XXX Coach".

In the health and wellness field, the biggest thing to watch out for liability wise is to not make any health diagnosis or promise of a cure for a specific health condition.

Most Health Coaches who follow this guideline should only buy limited liability insurance for less than $200 per year. (As of 2017)

Financial Coaching also has liability standards spelled out by the government for certain government certified specialties like the following:

- Chartered Financial Analyst (CFA) certification.
- Financial Risk Manager (FRM) Certification.
- Certified Financial Planner (CFP) Certification.
- Financial Modeling Certification.
- Certified Credit Professional (CCP)
- Chartered Global Management Accountant (CGMA)

In these government certified professions you need liability insurance or organizational agreements at the level of the risk you are operating at.

In fact Risk is a good way to look at legal liability overall.

Why You Should Become A Professional Coach

In the Medical Profession, if you give a patient treatment and it doesn't work well or kills them--you can be sued for millions of dollars.

As a Health Coach you are mainly making recommendations to your clients for them to work on their own lifestyle and health themselves. Therefore you have a much more limited liability— because the individual client is taking responsibility for themselves.

However, it is still a good idea to post lots of Medical and Health Liability statements for clients when coaching them so they are clear that they will be taking responsibility themselves to implement any suggestions you make to them.

Why You Should Become A Professional Coach

Why You Should Become A Professional Coach

Chapter 6: The Growth of Professional Coaching

The professional coaching industry is booming. Here is what one study says:

> Coaching is a booming international industry. In a global study released in 2012, the Lexington, Ky.-based International Coach Federation (ICF), the industry's largest trade association, estimated about 41,300 active professional coaches worldwide generated nearly $2 billion in annual revenue. In North America, about 14,060 coaches earned some $707 million.

I've seen other studies in 2017 which say that Coaching overall is growing about 13% per year. A pretty good rate—and this makes it an exciting profession to get into.

When you consider that there is really no "Barrier to Entry" to do coaching, then realistically anyone can hang out a shingle as a professional coach.

Your success is really dependent on your personal brand and how well you market and sell to your clients that they should use your services.

Given that "People" jobs are becoming more and more popular overall, and the growth in the number of niches for Coaching Professionals, this should be a good career option for many years to come.

Why You Should Become A Professional Coach

Chapter 7: Is Professional Coaching right for me?

You should ask yourself these questions:

- Do you like to help others?
- Do people like to tell you their problems or ask for your assistance?
- Are you willing to market yourself and your service to others?
- Are you good at feeling others pain and concerns?
- Do you want to run your own business even though the first years might be hard?

If the answers to the above questions are "Yes" then you would probably make a good professional coach.

You will also need to decide what type of Coach you want to be. As you can tell from previous chapters there are many options and it all comes down to your personal interests and background.

In Longevity Coaching (which is a type of health coaching), I often ask people to tell me about themselves.

If they have a variety of health and wellness related skills then they are a good fit for Longevity Coaching, because the integrated lifestyle we teach pulls everything together under one framework of wellness.

An example is a lady who was a Reiki Healer, Massage Therapist, and had many Spiritual interests. This made her decision to become a Longevity Coach easy because she saw that Longevity Coaching aligned with her personal interests and skills.

What about going from your existing job to becoming a Professional Coach?

In many cases you can get trained, certified, and even start seeing a few clients part time until you are ready to quit your existing job.

Coaching is something you can work into at your own pace.

Chapter 8: How to be successful as a Coach

Many people decide to become Coaches, get training, certified, then hang out a shingle.

Then they often fall on their faces and quit within a year

Based on my conversations over the last few years I would estimate that more than fifty percent of new coaches give up before they can make a good living at it.

I wasn't able to find any reliable statistics but the overall failure rate could be much higher.

Professional Coaching is almost always about running your own business, so you have to market and sell yourself successfully.

This means several things:

1) Building your own "Brand" based on your unique skillset
2) If you have an existing practice—how do your new skills integrate with the old ones?
3) Marketing yourself well at events, webinars, speaking engagements, and more
4) Selling potential clients on the value of your services. Usually by offering a first free session.

5) Setting your expectations realistically that it will take several years to grow a brand new Coaching business from scratch into something profitable.

6) Be persistent and don't give up. If you really believe that you have something to offer people, then they will eventually see it too.

You might also want to read my book: "Building a Successful Professional Coaching Business-Including a 90 Day Jumpstart Plan" to get more details on how to become successful as a professional coach.

Financial Health & Wellness

In addition, you should consider having multiple certifications which will help build your personal "Brand".

An example is a Longevity Coach working with people in their fifties and older.

Longevity Coaching is all about health & wellness, but considering the needs of your clients you might want to look outside the box for additional services to offer.

One of the big issues for many people is their financial health and wellness. So maybe you should consider adding certifications and products/services for those clients.

Then you could have revenue sources for the same clients which include those financial products and services as well as what you do for their long term health and happiness.

Why You Should Become A Professional Coach

Chapter 9: More on Business Planning for Success

Part of what I give to my Longevity Coaching candidates in the Coaching Course (which is part of their training) is a one hundred page Ebook on how they can build their business.

I'm not going repeat all of that here but I wanted to offer a few more pointers on being successful as a coach:

1) Do your planning and goal setting using "SMART" This is an acronym for Specific, Measurable, Achievable, Realistic, and Timely. All of your goals should reflect these principles. You can read online more about business planning. Basically you will be building a "Blueprint" for the business you are creating.

2) Build your personal brand by building an image you want everyone to think of you as when they contact you for coaching or your other related services. As an example, lets assume you have financial skills as well as health and wellness skills. Then maybe you would want to coach Baby Boomers and retirees who both need to have health and wellness as well as financial planning services.

3) Marketing is a subject we can take decades to cover, so lets just hit the highlights of what you want to build into your marketing:

Why You Should Become A
Professional Coach

a. A website is almost required these days to get the word out about your brand. You can find many free sites on the web to build one. (We also help our Coaches build their websites too)

b. Build a Social Media presence. You can start with a Facebook page, add Twitter, and many more Social media. It's not enough to just have a page, but you need to post regularly on things relevant to your brand.

c. This brings up a personal blog. Something you can build on your website. I have the world's largest Longevity Blog with over 900+ articles and growing weekly. This generates a lot of interest and traffic to my site.

d. Hold Webinars for potential clients. There are free and inexpensive tools on the web and it's a great way to build a following

e. Build your mailing list. These will be dedicated people who follow what you are doing and you can email them regularly. Use a site like AWeber or MailChimp to help you build your lists

f. Write an EBook and self publish it on Amazon.com A great way to build your personal credibility and get the word out.

g. Read some Books/EBooks on brand building and marketing. You can always learn more from others who have done it before.

There is a lot more you can do, and I lot more that I could discuss.

The main thing to keep in mind is that clients will not just come to you. You need to use these channels to find them.

I remember one "Coach" who was stuck on the idea that she just needed more certifications in more skills. She already had several certifications and had been doing training for years.

I tried to convince her that she really just needed to start her practice by working on her brand building and marketing to build a successful practice. (She didn't listen)

Why You Should Become A Professional Coach

Chapter 10: Virtual Coaching

The internet has enabled communications in our world in ways we could never have imagined a generation ago.

I talk with people all over the world every week, with both voice and images.

Tools like Skype, Google Hangouts, or Webinar tools are available on the Web all over the world, and these tools can be used by coaches too.

In the twentieth century personal coaching was almost always done in person.

Now, your personal "Brand" of coaching might be something of great interest for people all over your country, or even all over the world.

With Social Media and Email it's also much easier to attract interest about what you do for persons who are far away from the community where you live.

I use a lot of Social Media and Email in my business to notify people about Webinars which I hold once or twice each month.

Generating new customers through webinars is an exciting new avenue for my business.

Why You Should Become A Professional Coach

It's true that some wellness specialties have to be done in person like massages or other physical contact procedures.

However, many health and wellness specialties can be done remotely like Life Coaching, Remote Healing, and even Mindfulness Meditation sessions.

Anything which is all about talking with someone and having an interactive discussion, is something which lends itself well to the Virtual environment.

So in today's internet connected environment you will really be missing the boat if you don't have a Virtual strategy to serve remote customers as a large part of your business.

Of course I should also mention that Longevity Coaching lends itself well to working with Virtual clients since all the coaching and exercises can be done remotely.

Why You Should Become A Professional Coach

Chapter 11: How Your Age will affect your market:

You can decide to become a professional coach as a young adult or a senior building a new career after retiring from your original profession.

Your age will always be an important factor affecting your credibility with potential clients.

If you are twenty yours old trying to give a retired person health advice—you will be laughed at (or worse) very quickly. So you will need to have age relevant skills to market to your clients.

Let's use Longevity Coaching as an example

If you are younger (less than 35) talking to potential clients close to your age, you should focus on the "Personal Freedom" benefits of them learning the 10 Principles of Personal Longevity. This is since younger persons under 35 feel invincible and don't think about their longer term health, but they are open to coaching which will change how they look at the world.

On the other hand, if you are in your fifties or older, you will have a lot more credibility with your clients in talking about how to manage and improve your long term health.

I often tell my Longevity Coaching customers that the older they are—the more credibility they will have with their clients.

That when they reach one hundred they can fill a stadium to listen to them.

Overall, the type of coaching you offer, and your clients should be age focused based on how old you are and what your clients will be interested in.

Chapter 12: Additional Sources of Revenue

In addition to individual coaching you should also think about what additional revenue you can generate which will also help your clients

Multi-Level Marketing

I have positive and negative thoughts about multi-level marketing for a professional coach.

I've done multi-level marketing for some nutrition products—until I felt that I should make my business non-aligned with any particular supplier—to just focus on training.

However, I know several coaches who use nutritional suppliers with their coaching clients to offer additional help for those clients who need better eating habits, and they also benefit from those clients selling those nutrition products to others.

So for these people multi-level marketing works.

On the other hand selling the wrong products to coaching clients can hurt your credibility with them and pushing a particular product on a client might not be the best solution—although it's the only one you offer.

Lectures and Workshops

If you are comfortable speaking in front of groups then giving lectures and holding workshops might be a good addition to your personal brand.

Lectures and Workshops are a great way to build interest and credibility to generate new clients.

This is one reason we also market a Longevity Workshop Package to our coaching customers because we know that many of them both talk to groups and like to put on workshops and seminars for their clients.

Trade Shows

Trade show booths are often considered a form of marketing but they can also be another channel for working with clients too.

Having a booth at a trade show is best if you are offering specific products and services which are easy to quantify.

I've done lots of trade show booths in my life for various products and services.

The objective of a trade show booth is not to generate immediate sales (unless you have your whole store there)

It's mainly about generating interest and collecting sales leads you can follow up later.

Offering some type of prize or incentive to get people to leave you their contact information is a good way to go.

Doing good trade show booths is a whole "Artform" so you should think about whether this avenue is appropriate and affordable for your coaching business.

Chapter 13: Issues to watch out for:

Here are some issues to be careful about as you get into professional coaching…

<u>Lack of Support after Training</u>

One of the things that bothers me about the Industry is that many coaching training companies only seem to be interested in training and certifying their customers—then drop them.

I don't have any specific statistics but do talk to a lot of existing coaches who are dissatisfied with the companies which trained them and who don't get much support from their certifying organizations.

So one of the things to ask training and certifying organizations before you start is what type of support will they provide you after you finish your training and certification?

In my business I make additional efforts to help my clients such as:

1) Providing a Coaching course as part of Longevity training. The coaching course includes Ebooks on coaching, forms to use with clients, and a 100 page Ebook on how to build your business

2) Working with Longevity Coaches who have finished their training and certification to do marketing events with them to help them build their clients.

3) Having available associates of my company who specialize in helping coaches build their businesses-who I can connect my customers with.

Claims of Industry Certification

Since most of the Coaching business is unregulated, what claims are being made about how this particular Coaching program is certified? Who certifies it and where? Some of the claims vendors make might not be valid.

By the way, a University Certification for a Coaching program doesn't necessarily mean it's the right decision for you. You need to evaluate the whole package of services included.

Another factor is who has the knowledge and ability to certify a particular coaching program? My Longevity Coaching program is pretty "out of the box" so I maintain that only someone who has gone thru the full training would be qualified to certify it.

Anyone else trying to certify my Longevity Coaching program would be incompetent to do so.

How much does the Coaching Program cost?

Most Coaching Programs vary in price from $1,000 to $10,000. What is the value you will get for your money? Is the value really worth the money compared to the other options out there?

My own Longevity Coaching program currently charges a modest amount for full access. My approach is to charge less than some other coaching programs but also offer a lot more value. I have other options to offer customers, but overall I want to make sure I offer a lot more value than other programs people might consider.

(For Longevity Coaching current prices please check the "Prices" page on personal-longevity.com)

Can the Coaching program be paid for with Student Loans:

There might be exceptions, but since most professional coaching programs are new you will probably have to pay for them out of your own pocket.

Carefully follow up any claims that the training will be paid for by college/university financing to see that these claims are valid.

Why You Should Become A Professional Coach

Why You Should Become A Professional Coach

Chapter 14: Coaching Summary:

Overall, an investment in becoming a professional coach is a great idea for many people.

I talk with a lot of persons in their fifties and older looking for a new career.

They know that most traditional employers will not hire persons of their age, so they need to be creative and start something for themselves.

Professional Coaching is a good choice for these people.

If you make the right decisions and do good marketing, you certainly can make a great income at an older age.

In particular I know that most persons in this age group and older have lots of valuable experience and health/wellness skills which will provide lots of value for clients.

In fact the older a person becomes and stays healthy, the better candidate they are to become a Longevity Coach or other types of coaches—because they can teach others valuable life experience.

Many younger people have interests and passions to get into Coaching also. This can also be a great career choice in the slow economy we have had in the U.S. in the last ten years.

Whatever you decide I wish you all the best in your new career!

Marty Ettington

2017

Why You Should Become A
Professional Coach